JAMAICA

GROLIER EDUCATIONAL
SHERMAN TURNPIKE, DANBURY, CONNECTICUT 06816

EC PM LS

Published 1997 by Grolier Educational
Sherman Turnpike, Danbury, Connecticut.
Copyright © 1997 Marshall Cavendish Limited.

Set ISBN : 0-7172-9099-9
Volume ISBN : 0-7172-9114-6

Library of Congress Cataloging-in-Publication Data
Jamaica.
p.cm. -- (Fiesta!)
Includes index.
Summary: Discusses the festivals of Jamaica and how their songs, recipes, and traditions
reflect the culture of the people.
ISBN 0-7172-9114-6
1. Festivals -- Jamaica -- Juvenile literature. 2. Jamaica --Social life and customs -- Juvenile literature. [1.
Festivals -- Jamaica. 2. Holidays -- Jamaica. 3. Jamaica -- Social life and customs.]
I. Grolier Educational (Firm) II. Series: Fiesta! (Danbury, Conn.)
GT4827.A2J36 1997
394.2697292--DC21
97-11801
CIP
AC

Marshall Cavendish Limited
Editorial staff
Editorial Director: Ellen Dupont
Series Designer: Joyce Mason
Crafts devised and created by Susan Moxley
Music arrangements by Harry Boteler
Photographs by Bruce Mackie
Subeditors: Susan Janes, Judy Fovargue
Production: Craig Chubb

For this volume
Editor: Tessa Paul
Writer: Tim Cooke
Designer: Trevor Vertigan
Editorial Assistant: Lorien Kite
Consultant: Dr. Keith Nurse

Printed in Italy

Adult supervision advised for all crafts and recipes
particularly those involving sharp instruments and heat.

CONTENTS

Map of Jamaica 4

Religions and Greetings 6

Christmas 8

Story — Anansi 10

Jonkonnu 12

Easter 16

Fishermen's Festival 18

Harvest 22

National Heroes' Day 24

Story — A National Hero 26

Rastafarians 28

Words to Know 31
Set Contents 32

JAMAICA:

Set in the glittering Caribbean Sea, Jamaica is about 500 miles from the American mainland.

Cayman Islands

◀ **Beaches** in Jamaica attract tourists from all over the world. Palm trees provide shade from the tropical sun.

▼ **Kingston** is the capital of Jamaica. Devon House, in Kingston, is one of the finest old buildings in the country.

▼ **Seafood**, such as fresh fish and lobster, is used in Jamaican cooking. Fish preserved in salt is also popular. Jamaicans often make spicy curries.

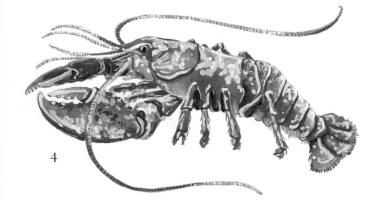

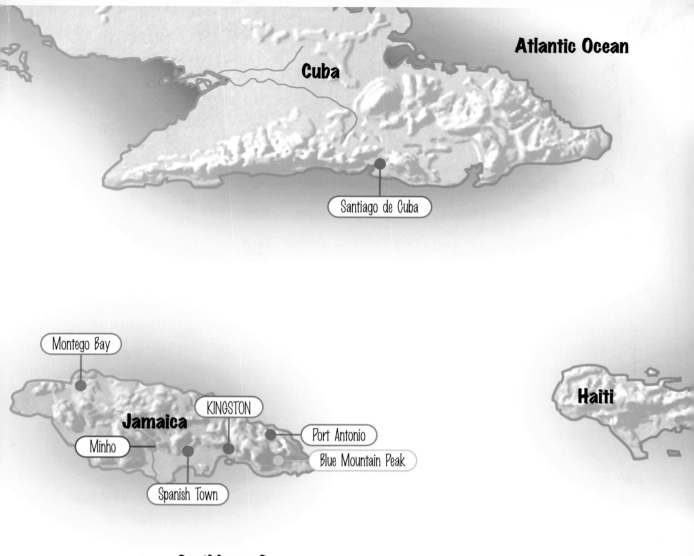

Atlantic Ocean

Cuba

Santiago de Cuba

Haiti

Montego Bay

Jamaica

KINGSTON

Minho

Port Antonio

Blue Mountain Peak

Spanish Town

Caribbean Sea

▶ **Christian churches** in
Jamaica are crowded with believers.
Many other Jamaicans are Rastafarians.
They say that it is God's will for them one
day to settle in Ethiopia, eastern Africa.

RELIGIONS

The majority of Jamaicans are Christian. The Protestant churches have the biggest following. There are also Roman Catholics and some cults that mix old African beliefs with Christianity.

Christopher Colombus sailed from Spain and landed on Jamaica in 1494. He admired the beautiful island, and he claimed it for the King and Queen of Spain.

Spaniards settled on the island. Spanish priests, who were members of the Roman Catholic Church, came too. The merchants started to bring African slaves to work in Jamaica, and the priests introduced them to Christianity. But the greatest influence in the growth of Jamaica came from the English. They took Jamaica from Spain in

The crucifix is an important image in Christianity. It indicates the death of Christ and His suffering for the world. Christians believe that Christ died so that humans could have life after death.

1655, and with these new rulers arrived new Christian priests who belonged to the Church of England. Many Jamaicans are still faithful to the Church of England. Their hymns and carols are from a common hymn book shared by Church of England people all over the world, and the same services are followed.

There are various other Christian sects on the island. Some show the heritage of Africa in their services. The music has an African rhythm, and the services are informal, with people singing their own songs of praise.

Some belong to groups with European roots, such as the Baptists and Methodists, which originated in England.

The Syrian community, who

came as traders to Jamaica early this century, is Roman Catholic. This is a small group, but powerful, wealthy, and educated. One of Jamaica's first prime ministers came from Syrian stock.

A small Jewish community lives on the island. They escaped from persecution in Europe and felt at ease in Jamaica, where the islanders are tolerant of religious differences.

A new sect has emerged in recent years. Its faith is rooted in the Bible and inspires black people to overcome the slavery of the past. This is the Rastafarian movement.

Rastafarians refer to the writings of Ancient Egypt to support their beliefs. They look to the Egyptian "Book of the Dead" where they find mention of the Rastafarian people. Their name comes from the Prince Rasta Fari. whom they regard as their spiritual leader. He later became Haile Selassie, Emperor of Ethiopia in Africa.

GREETINGS FROM **JAMAICA!**

Jamaicans speak English, and English is the country's official language. But the language of the island, just like its history and culture, has been shaped by many different peoples. Most Jamaicans speak a creole derived from English, French, Spanish, and African languages. Some words survive from the days of the Spaniards or the French, and the Indians before that have also left their mark. Most Jamaicans are descended from African slaves, who brought many of their own words and expressions to the language. When people are with their friends or families, they speak a very Jamaican type of English and use many of these expressions. But in formal situations they use the type of English spoken all over the world.

About 80 percent of the people are Christians — Anglicans, Baptists, members of the Church of God, and Roman Catholics. There are also Jewish, Hindu, and Muslim communities.

CHRISTMAS

Christmas in Jamaica is a time for theater and musical shows, as well as gifts and parties.

Many parts of a Jamaican Christmas date back to when the British ruled the island. Turkey is eaten on Christmas Day, as are British Christmas plum puddings and cakes. Santa Claus brings presents, and houses are decorated with Christmas trees and nativity scenes.

Christmas is time for pantomimes, a type of British musical show following traditional plots that are based on old fairy tales. In Jamaica these include local folk tales about a little spider named Anansi. Theaters and dance companies are also

AWAY IN A MANGER

A - way in a — man - ger, no — crib for a bed, The — lit - tle Lord Je - sus laid — down His sweet head; The stars in the — bright sky looked — down where he lay, The — lit - tle Lord Je - sus a - sleep on the hay.

very busy at this time of year. Church, carol-singing, and theater are all vital to the enjoyment of a true Jamaican Christmas.

The Christmas pudding is similar to that found in Britain, but richer and spicier. Trinkets are used to decorate the Christmas tree.

GINGERBREAD

MAKES 15 SLICES

1 stick butter, plus 1 tbsp for greasing bread pan
½ cup molasses
⅔ cup packed light brown sugar
2½ cups all-purpose flour
2 tsp baking powder
2 tsp ground ginger
½ tsp salt
¼ tsp ground nutmeg
2 eggs, beaten
1 cup milk
1 tsp grated fresh ginger

1 Heat oven to 350°F. Grease a 9 x 5 in bread pan.
2 Put 1 stick butter, molasses, and sugar in a saucepan over low heat. Stir until sugar melts. Turn off heat, and leave until cool.
3 Sift flour, baking powder, ground ginger, salt, and nutmeg into bowl.
4 Add eggs and milk to pan. Pour the liquid into the bowl. Mix well. Stir in fresh ginger.
5 Spoon batter into bread pan and smooth top. Bake 50 minutes or until a skewer inserted in middle comes out clean.
6 Let gingerbread cool in pan on wire rack. Serve in slices.

ANANSI

The character of Anansi the spider was brought to Jamaica

by West African slaves. He has become a familiar character,

and there are always new stories about him.

Parents tell Anansi stories to their children at bedtime, and at

Christmas time children's theater feature Anansi.

ON THE DAY OF King Leo's costume party Anansi spent many hours making a knight's suit of armor. He used old pots and pans to make it. But the suit was too heavy to wear while walking the long road to the party. He hid the suit under a hedge near Leo's house. Rabbit and Bear saw the little spider hiding his clever suit of armor.

"I like that costume," sniggered Bear, picking up the suit. A few hours later Anansi crept back to the bush. He wore only a small sheet tied around his waist. He was furious to find his armor gone. Then he saw his old friends, the jokers Rabbit and Bear, struggling to get into a donkey suit. Bear was too big to squeeze into the back legs, and Rabbit could not fit the head over his huge ears. At last they got into the donkey suit, and they stumbled across Farmer George's carrot field.

Anansi ran as quickly as he could to the farmhouse. "Farmer George!" he shouted. "Your donkey's eating your carrots!" The farmer jumped up and grabbed a big stick. Farmer George started beating the donkey and then locked it in his stable.

"I'll go to the party anyway," decided Anansi, "and tell the others that I forgot it was a costume party."

But when he arrived, King Leo came and clapped him on the back before Anansi had a chance to say a word. "Anansi," said the lion, "what a great costume. You are clever to come as a cute little baby!" Anansi had forgotten he was wearing only a small white sheet. King Leo thought it was a diaper! All the other animals thought it was funny, but Anansi won the prize for his costume.

JONKONNU

On the day after Christmas Jamaicans celebrate Jonkonnu, a festival with roots going back to the days of the slave trade.

Jonkonnu parades dance through the streets. Everyone wears a mask and a colorful costume.

This day falls on the day immediately after Christmas. It was the one day that slaves on the old plantations of Jamaica did not have to work. It was the only chance they had to enjoy themselves. The festival was the slaves' way of remembering their roots in Africa. Some people say that the Jonkonnu festival takes its name from John Canoe, an African slave trader.

The slaves used the carnival to make fun of those in charge. Teasing the slave owners and their wives, they imitated their way of walking and talking.

These days carnival costumes portray characters from stories and myths. Cows, horses, warriors, kings, and queens appear, as well as a frightening figure of the devil, dressed all in black.

SLY MONGOOSE

Sly Mon-goose, —— your name gone a-broad, Sly Mon-goose —

— your name gone a-broad. Mon-goose slip in-to

Bed-ward kit-chen, Steal out one of his right-eous chick-en,

Put it in-to his waist-coat pock-et, Sly Mon-goose.

Many carnivals in the Caribbean are huge affairs. Jonkonnu is a quieter, family parade. But the drums play, whistles shriek, and everyone shakes tassels and feathers while they sing and dance.

MAKE A HEADDRESS

Carnival headdresses are works of art. They can be elaborate and very heavy. But it is easy to make a colorful headdress that is bright and easy to wear.

Street parades or carnivals in the West Indies have become huge events. Thousands of tourists go to see the fantastic costumes. The people wearing these outfits have spent months making them. Many bands fill the air with music. Often the musicians are professional players.

Jonkonnu in Jamaica is very much part of the Christmas season, but it is enjoyed most in the villages and country towns. Children dress up for the joyful procession. They wear costumes and sing and dance. Country headdresses are made at home. People use cardboard and paint and glue to make their own designs.

This is a grand headdress. The arches on either side frame the face like a picture. The top can grow high and spectacular. Just add a few feathers and tassels or ribbons and raffia for an original Jonkonnu headpiece. Some artists might like to use shells and leaves for a true country look.

The colors in this headdress copy the flowers of Jamaica. The red of the hibiscus and the pink of orchids create an eye-catching design.

1 Cut two lengths of cardboard about 4 inches wide and 18 inches long. On one edge of each length curve two corners as shown. This makes the double-layered crossbar. Cut two more lengths 3 inches wide and 12 inches long. On one corner of each cut a curve to match the curves on the crossbar. On the other corner make a long curve. These make the two side frames. Slip side frames into crossbar, matching top curves; glue in place. Glue, then staple, outer edges together, leaving a bottom opening. Reinforce curved corners with masking tape.

YOU WILL NEED
Sheets of cardboard or a cardboard box • Stapler • Tape Poster paint • Glue • Feathers Tinsel •Ribbons • Sequins

2 You now have a basic headdress structure. The crossbar opens to fit your head. Give the whole structure a thick, smooth cover of poster paint. Make tassels from crepe paper or ribbons to glue to the structure. Glue on sequins, feathers, tinsel, ribbons, and buttons. Have fun making your own design and color scheme.

EASTER

As in other parts of the Christian world, Easter in Jamaica is a solemn time followed by a day of rejoicing.

For all Christians Easter marks the death of Christ and His resurrection, or rising from the dead. Jamaicans take the festival very seriously. After Christmas Easter is the most important holiday of the year.

Forty days before Good Friday of Easter Christians celebrate Ash Wednesday. They go to church, where the priest smears their foreheads with ash. This is a sign that they are sorry for any wrong they did in the past year. It also prepares them for the days of Lent. This is the time to give up favorite foods and pleasures in memory of Christ.

The first service of Easter is held on Good Friday, which is said to be the day on which Jesus was crucified. At midday everyone goes to church. Services on Good Friday may last up to three hours.

After church all the people go home for a quiet

The night before Jesus was taken away to His death He had a last supper with His close friends, the twelve disciples. He blessed the bread and wine on the table before He served it. Christians remember this act. In their church services they are given bread and wine blessed by the priest. The carving shows the Last Supper.

evening. This is a sad day for Christians.

Sunday is the day for celebrating Christ's resurrection. Children are given Easter eggs and chocolate bunnies. Festive food is served to the family. The next day, Monday, is a day off for all to enjoy.

Church candles are not lighted on Good Friday. This is the day when Christians recall the death of Christ on the cross. On Sunday the candles are lighted. Dark bread, called bun, and cheese are eaten. Chocolate eggs and special foods are enjoyed.

FISHERMEN'S FESTIVAL

Jamaica's brightly painted fishing boats are one of the prettiest sights on the island. But the Caribbean, like other seas, can be dangerous. Once a year the fishermen ask Saint Peter to keep them safe at sea.

The sea plays a key role in the history and life of Jamaica. The first Europeans in Jamaica stormed the island from their sailing ships. Other ancestors of modern Jamaicans survived a long, terrible voyage across the ocean after they had been torn from their homes in Africa to become slaves on the island.

Many Jamaicans rely on the sea to earn their living. There are fishermen and sailors, and others who sell the fish. On June 29 the islanders celebrate their ties with the sea. This day is the day of Saint Peter, the patron saint of fishermen.

A patron saint is a saint who is believed to look after a certain group of people. Peter became one of Jesus's greatest disciples, and

The plants that grow on Jamaica are colorful and bright. The beaches are scattered with interesting shells. Fishermen use both to decorate their boats for the festival.

*Saint Peter is an important disciple.
After Jesus died, he taught people
about the Christian faith.
In heaven he is believed to hold the
keys to the Kingdom of God.*

he was once a fisher-
man. When Saint Peter
began to gather fol-
lowers for the new
religion of Christianity,
his converts called him
"the Fisher of Men."

No one fishes on
the day of the festival
of Saint Peter. Early
in the morning the
brightly colored boats
of the islanders are
pulled up onto the
beach. The fishermen
hang beautiful flowers
over their boats.

The priest comes
to the beach, where he
blesses the boats and
offers prayers to Saint
Peter. He asks him to
protect the fishermen
when they are at sea.

WEAVE A FISH

These colorful fish are woven from strips of thick paper. Attach string to create bright mobiles, or use them as wall hangings.

This project combines two major aspects of Jamaican life — the sea and craftwork. Many islanders rely on the sea for a living. Some are sailors; others are fishermen. And there are the traders who sell the fish. When the boats come ashore at the end of the day, the fishmongers will be waiting for them. Large baskets, woven on the island, are used to carry the fish to the market stalls and shops. Weaving is an old craft, brought centuries ago from Africa.

These fish were made from thick paper that had been dappled with color before it was cut into strips. Mark the fins with paint, and color in the eyes and mouth.

YOU WILL NEED
Sheet of thick paper
Ruler
A pair of scissors
Poster paint (optional)

20

Horizontals

ticals

1 Cut thick paper into 15 strips. Each strip should be about 1 inch wide and about 18 inches long. Lay out seven strips vertically. From the top measure 2 inches. From this point, start to weave horizontal rows from the remaining eight strips. The horizontal rows must have a 2-inch overhang on the left. Now you will have a woven piece with eight horizontal strips and seven vertical strips. On the top and the left the strips show 2 inches of unwoven paper.

2 Counting from the left, choose the fifth vertical strip. Take the long end. Fold it to the left at an angle, then weave it through the horizontal strips. It will form a ninth horizontal. Count from the top to the sixth horizontal. Fold upward at an angle. Weave it to form an eighth vertical. Working at the upper edge, fold each 2-inch end of the vertical strips, and tuck each neatly into the horizontals. Working on the left side, take each short 2-inch end of the horizontal strips, and tuck each into the verticals. You will have woven one right-angled corner.

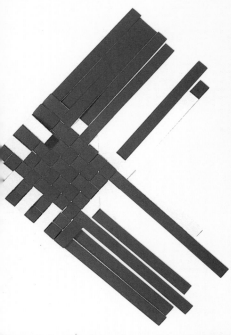

3 Count from left to the fifth vertical. Fold the long end of the seventh vertical at an angle toward the left, and weave into horizontals. Count from the top, and fold the sixth horizontal at an angle upward, and weave into verticals. Fringe the ends of the unwoven strips by cutting each end into numerous short strips. Wrap these fringed ends tightly around a pencil, then with a hard tug pull the pencil free. This will give the fish tail a loose, curled look.

HARVEST

In Jamaica, as in many other countries, the end of the harvest is the time for going to church to give thanks. The rich soil of the island has provided food for the coming year.

At the end of the year's harvest the Jamaicans celebrate with a special festival in church. The ceremony is similar to the harvest festivals in most Christian states. Jamaicans take the harvest very seriously. The island depends on farming. In the past, if all the crops failed, everyone had a difficult winter. So the end of the harvest is a time to rest and give thanks to God.

People choose the best crops and use them to decorate their church. They hang up palm leaves and banana branches. Displays of fruit and vegetables are put before the altar.

On Harvest Sunday everyone can be found in church. Next day the produce is sold at street stalls. Bands play, and people are in party mood now that the hard farm work is over.

SPINACH SALAD

SERVES 4 TO 6

6 slices bacon
1 papaya or pawpaw
⅓ cup olive oil
3 tbsp white wine vinegar
1 tsp mustard
Salt and pepper
¾ pound young fresh spinach
1 cup cashews, toasted

1 Ask an adult to broil bacon until crisp. Drain bacon on paper towels. Cut into small pieces.
2 Also ask adult to peel papaya and cut it into quarters. Remove seeds. Thinly slice papaya; set aside.
3 Put olive oil, vinegar, mustard, and salt and pepper in a jar, and screw on lid. Shake jar several times to make a dressing; set aside.
4 Tear spinach leaves from stems. Rinse spinach leaves in a sink of cold water several times until all dirt and grit are removed. Drain well and pat dry with several paper towels.
5 Put spinach leaves in a salad bowl. Sprinkle bacon and cashew nuts on top.
6 Shake dressing again. Pour dressing over salad. Toss all ingredients together and serve.

Jamaicans balance food on their heads as they go to market or the harvest festivities. All give thanks for the rich island crops.

NATIONAL HEROES' DAY

Every year Jamaicans recall their past. They honor the African people who suffered the bondage of slavery on the island's sugar plantations. The leaders who fought for freedom are remembered.

One of the most important dates in the history of Jamaica is 1834. That was when slavery was abolished by the island's British rulers. The event is celebrated every year on the third Monday in October. The festival is known as National Heroes' Day and also as African Emancipation Day. The heroes are all the people who fought for an end to slavery. "Emancipation" means setting free.

Heroes' Day is a public holiday. People join in all sorts of celebrations. This is the day when those Jamaicans who have served their country well in the past year receive awards from the government. The popular way to spend the day is by taking an excursion. Groups hire buses and go to the beach or go out in the country for the whole day.

Everyone prepares picnic food. The fun and dancing go on all day and all through the night.

Africans brought their own ways with them. They carved and made buckets from gourds. They grew fruits they knew from home. The islanders have kept these ways.

TROPICAL SALAD

SERVES 4 TO 6

2 pink grapefruits
2 large avocados
1 tsp sugar
1 tsp mustard
1 garlic clove, peeled and
crushed
¼ cup grapefruit juice
⅓ cup olive oil
Salt and pepper
Fresh parsley, to garnish

1 Ask an adult to seed and peel avocados and segment grapefruits.

2 Cut avocado halves into thin slices. Arrange avocado and grapefruits on a serving platter.

3 Put the remaining ingredients, except parsley, in a jar, and screw on lid. Shake the jar to make a dressing.

4 Pour dressing over salad. Cover and chill until ready to serve. Garnish with fresh parsley.

A NATIONAL HERO

Nanny is one of Jamaica's seven National Heroes – people

honored for their part in the struggle for freedom. She led the

Windward Maroons, a group of ex-slaves who had escaped to the

remote Blue Mountains.

NANNY GREW UP on the Gold Coast of West Africa, which is today known as Ghana. She was a member of the Ashanti tribe. Like most of the Ashantis, Nanny was a skilled warrior. Her people were famous for their bravery.

When Nanny was still young, she was captured and sold into slavery. She was forced onto a slave ship and taken to Jamaica. The sea journey lasted for three months. The slaves were not given enough food or water, and many of them died. When the ship finally arrived in Jamaica, the survivors were taken to work on a large sugar planta-tion. Life was hard in the sugarcane

fields. Every day Nanny and the other slaves worked from dawn till dusk. The slave masters were cruel, especially to the women. Nanny was a proud, strong woman and felt great anger at this life.

The slaves comforted each other by telling stories about the Maroons, slaves who had escaped and now lived as free men and women in the mountains. One day Nanny escaped and went off in search of these brave people. Eventually she found them, high in the Blue Mountains. With her military skills Nanny was able to help the Maroons defend themselves against the British. The Maroons were so impressed that they made her their queen. Under her leadership the Maroons began a series of fierce attacks on the sugar plantations. They helped many slaves to escape.

After long years of fighting the British realized that they would never defeat Nanny. They agreed to stop attacking her people. They, too, recognized her as a queen.

RASTAFARIANS

The Rastafarians have created a new form of Christianity. Although a minority in Jamaica, they have had a great influence on the island.

In the 1930s a group of Jamaicans grew unhappy with the Christian religion. They thought it did not do much to help black people. When they studied their Bibles, they found clues that led them to a new interpretation.

They said that the emperor of Ethiopia, in Africa, was the new messiah. His name was Ras Tafari. The people who followed him became known as Rastafarians, or Rastas. In later years the emperor took the title Haile Selassie.

The new religion began at a time when many black people were growing more interested in their African roots. A Jamaican called Marcus Garvey took up these ideas, and he

The Lion of Zion is the image of a brave, proud creature. Rastas try to have these qualities, too. A badge shows Marcus Garvey in a splendid helmet. Garvey's work inspired the Rastafarian movement. The Rastas have their own flag. It is a public sign of their faith.

started a movement called the Universal Negro Improvement Association. He said that black people should be proud of their roots and seek to return to Africa.

The Rastas read the same message in the Bible. They were all descendants of the old kings of Ethiopia, they believed. One day they would all return to that country from their exile.

Haile Selassie was sometimes called Jah, or God. He was also known as the Lion of Judah. Rastas have adopted the image of the lion. They let their hair grow into long dreadlocks like a lion's mane, and they walk proudly like lions.

Rastas wear the colors of the Ethiopian flag: red, green, and gold. They spend a lot

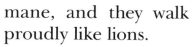

The Egyptian birdwoman recalls the roots of the Rastas. They believe their tribe is mentioned in the 5,000-year-old Book of the Dead and comes from Ancient Egypt. Hats and bags carry Rasta symbols.

29

of time reading the Bible, and they are peaceful people. They meditate to the sound of drums and chants.

Although Rastas are only a minority in Jamaica, they are a major part of how people see the island. This is partly because the reggae singer Bob Marley used his songs to spread their beliefs. The religion is closely tied to reggae music.

There are three main types of Rastafarians, varying from the very traditional to the more modern. All Rastafarians celebrate holy days in private, at home with the family or at church.

Their celebrations follow the Christian calendar. Rastafarians also honor the day on which their messiah Haile Selassie became an emperor and his birthday on July 23.

Although Rastafarians do not have big, noisy celebrations, they are eager to show their religion. Badges, flags, and even watches carry images of faith. Haile Selassie is their messiah. His face appears on many items. The reggae singer Bob Marley is honored as a missionary.

WORDS TO KNOW

Abolish: To put an end to a way of doing things.

Altar: A table on which worshipers leave offerings, burn incense, or perform ceremonies.

Anansi: A spider character from African folk tales. Anansi fables are popular as children's bedtime stories.

Creole: A language that is a mixture of European and other languages, usually African.

Exile: A time spent away from the country of one's birth, against one's wishes.

Jonkonnu: This Jamaican holiday takes place on the day after Christmas. Slaves on the old plantations started Jonkonnu as a way of recalling their African roots. The festival is celebrated with costume parades featuring traditional folk characters.

Messiah: According to the Bible, the holy person who will set people free from suffering. Most Christians believe that Jesus Christ was the Messiah, but the Rastafarian sect believes differently.

Pantomime: A funny musical play based on a fairy tale. Staging pantomimes at Christmas is a British tradition that has taken hold in Jamaica.

Plantation: A large farm that usually grows just one crop. The workers on a plantation usually live on its land.

Rastafarianism: A Jamaican religious sect whose followers regard the former Emperor of Ethiopia, Haile Selassie, as the Messiah. Rastafarians believe that they are desccended from Ethiopian kings, and that they will one day return to that country.

Reggae: A type of Jamaican music, it is a combination of traditional Jamaican music, rock and roll, and soul. It has a strong back beat.

Sect: A group of people within a religion whose beliefs differ from those of the other members.

Slave: A person who is, by law, owned by another person. The law requires a slave to obey the orders of his or her owner.

ACKNOWLEDGMENTS

WITH THANKS TO:

Chensie Chen, candelabra p16-17. Fats Restaurant, Shirland Road, London, garland p8-9, steel drum p12, decorated gourd p24. Pollock's Toy Museum, London dolls p22. Vale Antiques, London Saint Peter carving p19.

PHOTOGRAPHS BY:

All photographs by Bruce Mackie. Cover photograph by ZEFA.

ILLUSTRATIONS BY:

Fiona Saunders title page, p4-5, Mountain High Maps ® Copyright © 1993 Digital Wisdom, Inc. p4-5. Philip Divine p7. Tony Ross p10-11.

SET CONTENTS

BRAZIL
Festa de Iemanjá 8
Lavagem do Bonfim 10
Carnival 12
Festas Juninas 18
Festa do 20 de Setembro 22
Christmas 26
Bumba-meu-boi 28

CHINA
Chinese New Year 8
Qing Ming 16
Dragon Boat Festival 20
Moon Festival 22
Chong Yang 26
Miao Festivals 28

GERMANY
Advent 8
Christmas 12
New Year 16
Fasching 18
Easter 20
May Day 24
Saint Martin's Day 26
Driving Down the Cattle 30

INDIA
Pongal Harvest Festival 8
Holi Festival 10
Baisakhi – A Sikh Festival 12
Raksha Bandhan 14
Janmashtami – Krishna's Birthday 16
Ganesha Festival 20
Navratri and Dasara 22
Divali 26
Eid-ul-Fitr – A Muslim Festival 28

IRELAND
Christmas 8
Easter 12
Saint Patrick's Day 14
Lammas day 20
Puck Fair 22
All Souls' Day 28

ISRAEL
Rosh Hashanah 8
Sukkot 10
Simkhat Torah 12

Chanukah 14
Tu Bishvat 18
Purim 20
Pesakh 24
Yom Ha'atzma'ut 28

ITALY
Christmas 8
Carnevale 12
Easter 14
Raduno 16
Palio 18
Ferragosto 20
Saint Francis 22
Olive Festival 26
Festa dei Morti 28
Stella Maris 30

JAMAICA
Christmas 8
Jonkonnu 12
Easter 16
Fishermen's Festival 18
Harvest 22
National Heroes' Day 24
Rastafarians 28

JAPAN
New Year Festival 8
Setsubun 14
Cherry Blossom Celebrations 16
Doll Festival 18
Children's Day 20
Shrine Festivals 22
Star Festival 24
Obon Festival 26
Shichi-Go-San 28

KOREA
Solnal 8
Buddha's Birthday 12
Tano 18
Chusok 20
Han-gul Day 26
Andong Folk Festival 28

MEXICO
Holy Week 8
Independence Day 10
Days of the Dead 12
Our Lady of Guadalupe 18

Christmas 20
Saints' Days 24
Huichol Festivals 28

NIGERIA
Leboku 8
Fishing Festival 12
Mmanwe Festival 14
Regatta 18
Osun Ceremony 20
Sallah 24
Christmas 28
Independence Day 30

PERU
Virgin of Candelaria 8
Holy Week 10
Fiesta del Cruz 12
Qoyllur Rit'i 16
Corpus Christi 18
Inti Raymi 20
Illapu 24
Dia del Puno 26

RUSSIA
Christmas 8
Festival of Winter 10
New Year 16
Women's Day 20
Victory Day 24
Easter 28
Revolution Day 30

TURKEY
Birth of the Prophet 8
Kurban Bayrami 10
Iftar Meal 16
Sheker Bayrami 18
Lélé-I-Mirach 20
Asure Gunu 24
Aksu Black Sea Festival 26
Mesir Paste 28
Atatürk 30

VIETNAM
Ong Tao Festival 8
Tet – New Year's Day 10
Ho Lim Festival 16
Hung Temple Festival 20
Ho Chi Minh's Birthday 24
Vu Lan Day 26
Tet Trung Thu 28